Fun to Draw

Cover illustrated by Tanya Kornikova
Illustrated by Tiphanie Beeke, Michelle Berg, Kallen Godsey,
Robin Moro, Ryan Sias, and David Wojtowycz

Photography by Siede Preis Photography and Brian Warling Photography

Copyright © 2010 Publications International, Ltd. All rights reserved.

This publication may not be reproduced in whole or in part by any means
whatsoever without written permission from

Louis Weber, C.E.O.
Publications International, Ltd.
7373 North Cicero Avenue
Lincolnwood, Illinois 60712
Ground Floor, 59 Gloucester Place
London W1U 8JJ

Permission is never granted for commercial purposes.

Customer Service: 1-800-595-8484 or customer_service@pilbooks.com

www.pilbooks.com

p i kids is a trademark of Publications International, Ltd., and is registered in the United States.

8 7 6 5 4 3 2 1

Manufactured in China.

ISBN-13: 978-1-60553-749-8
ISBN-10: 1-60553-749-7

Welcome!

This Fun to Draw workbook has been specially designed to help prepare your child for school. You and your child should work together on each activity. In the front of the book, you will find simple, introductory exercises. As you work your way to the back of the book, the exercises will gradually become more complex and challenging.

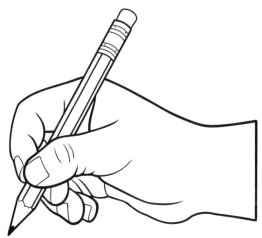

Before you begin, show your child how to hold a pencil properly. Your child should pinch the pencil between the thumb and index finger. The side of the pencil should rest against the side of the middle finger. As your child practices drawing this way, they will build important fine motor skills.

As children gain fine motor skills, they build strength in the small muscles in their hands. Activities that require fine motor skills, such as coloring and drawing, develop the accuracy and control children need in order to learn to write. Building these important skills helps prepare your child for school.

In addition to developing fine motor skills, the exercises in this book will challenge your child to distinguish shapes, practice counting, and follow simple directions. To make the most of each activity, keep these suggestions in mind:

• Tear out the page along the perforation and lay it flat on your work surface. This will help your child focus on just one activity at a time.

• Read the directions aloud.

• Let your child attempt each activity and only assist when necessary.

• Be positive and encouraging. Learning should be fun!

When you reach the end of the workbook, celebrate your child's accomplishments. Remove the certificate of achievement and write your child's name on it so they can proudly display it.

Certificate of Achievement

I can DRAW!
Congratulations!

Taylor
(name)

has successfully completed the FUN TO DRAW workbook

Presented on **June 12**

Presented by **Mom**

Straight Lines
Follow the paths.

Start on the green dot and stop on the red dot.

Square

Trace the shapes.

blocks

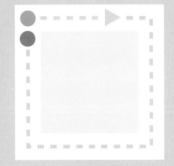

house

fish tank

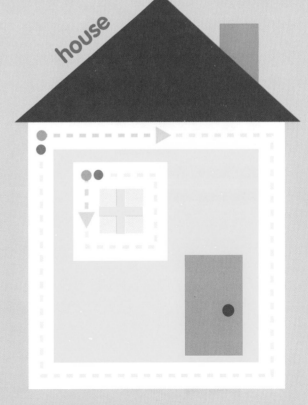

Rectangle

Trace the shapes.

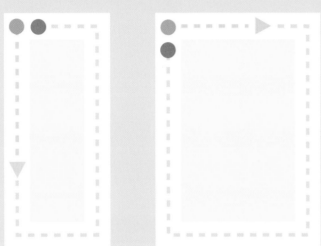

flag

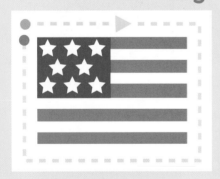

flower box

train cars

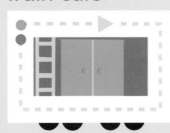

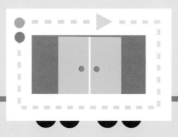

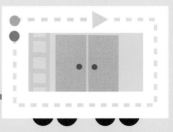

Diamond

Trace the shapes.

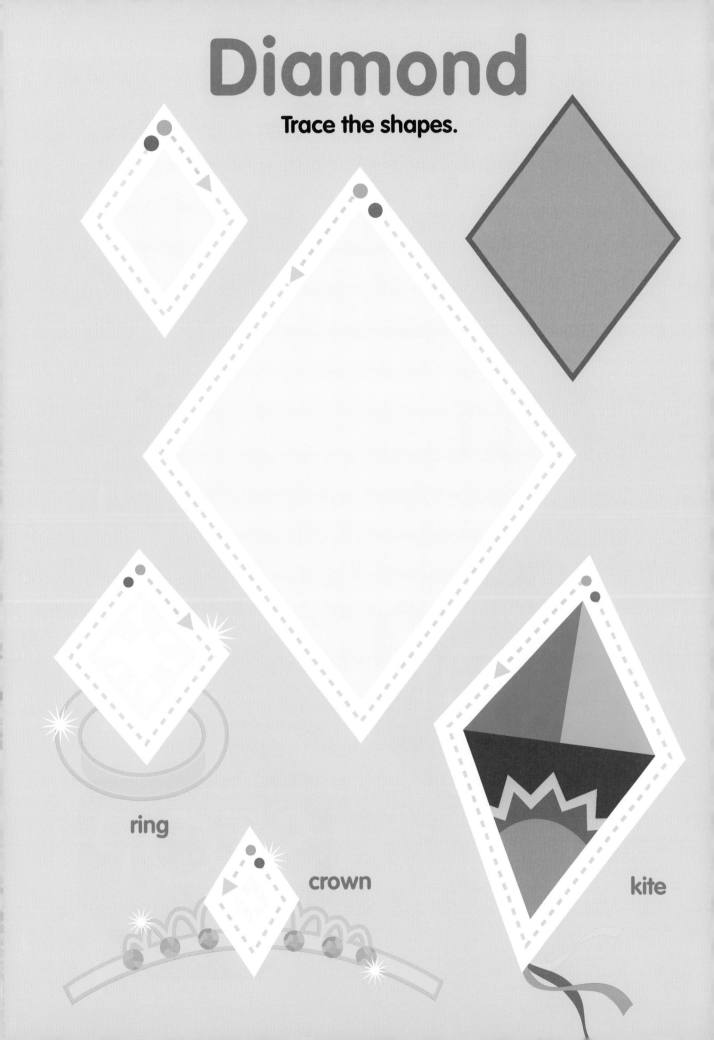

ring

crown

kite

Octagon

Trace the shapes.

Heart

Trace the shapes.

1 one

Draw one butterfly.

2 two

Draw two airplanes.

3 three

Draw three trees.

Draw four buildings.

5 five

Draw five stars.

Draw six flower petals.

7 seven

Draw seven apples.

8 eight

Draw eight windows.

9 nine

Draw nine balloons.

10 ten

Draw ten candles.

Let's Draw Fish!

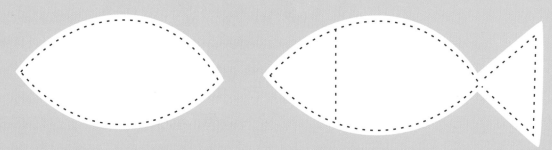

1. To begin, draw the body.

2. Next, add a head and a tail.

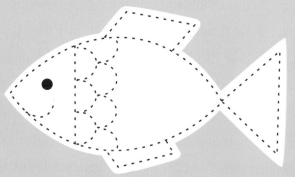

3. Finally, add fins, an eye, and a mouth. Add scales if you want!

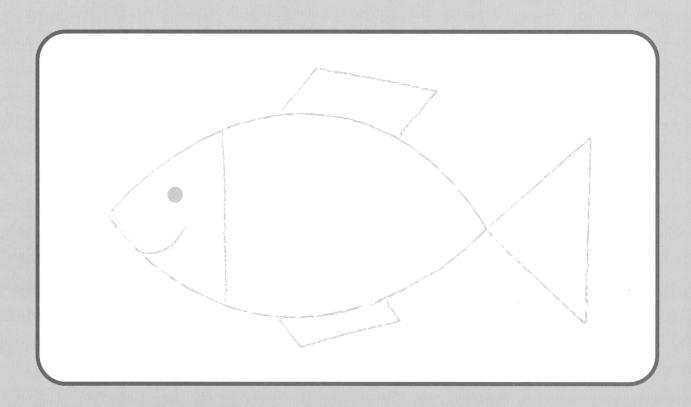

Draw some fish in the water.

Let's Draw a Sailboat!

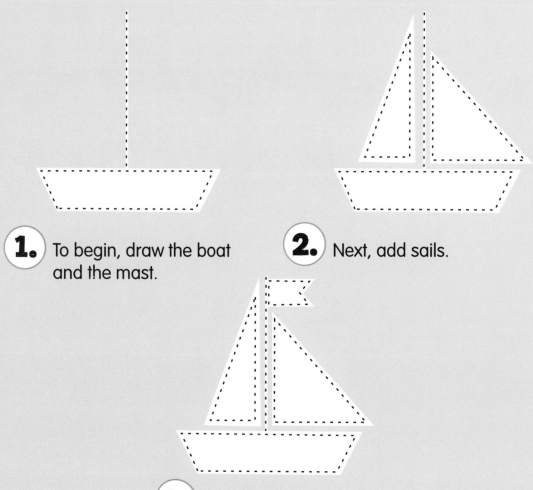

1. To begin, draw the boat and the mast.

2. Next, add sails.

3. Finally, add a flag.

Draw some sailboats in the water.

Let's Draw an Airplane!

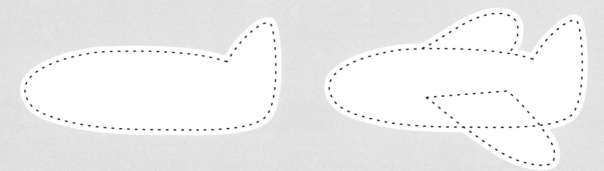

1. First, draw the body.

2. Next, add wings.

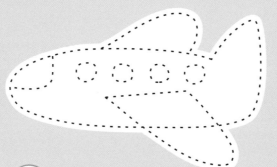

3. Finally, add windows.

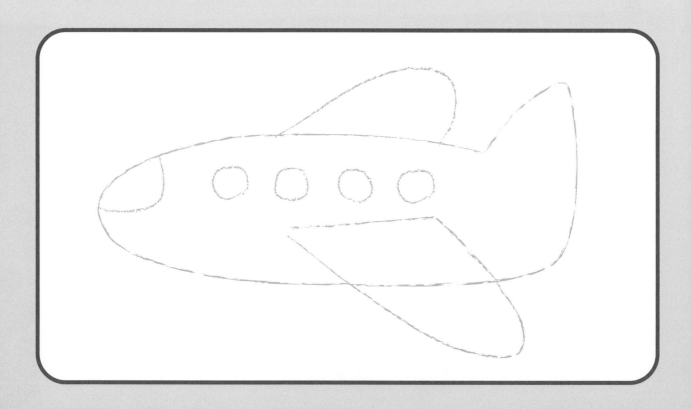

Draw an airplane in the sky.

Let's Draw an Ant!

1. To begin, draw the body.

2. Next, add a face.

3. Finally, add legs and antennae.

Draw some ants in the grass.

Let's Draw a Boy!

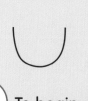

1. To begin, draw a jaw. It looks like a **U**.

2. Next, add hair.

3. Then, add a face and ears.

4. Draw the body.

5. Draw arms and legs.

6. Finally, add hands and feet.

Draw a boy in the field.
Is he with a friend?

Let's Draw a Girl!

1. To begin, draw a jaw. It looks like a **U**.

2. Next, add hair.

3. Then, draw a face.

4. Draw the body.

5. Add a skirt.

6. Draw the arms.

7. Now, draw legs.

8. Finally, add hands and feet.

Draw a girl by the flowers.
Is she with a friend?

Let's Draw a Skyscraper!

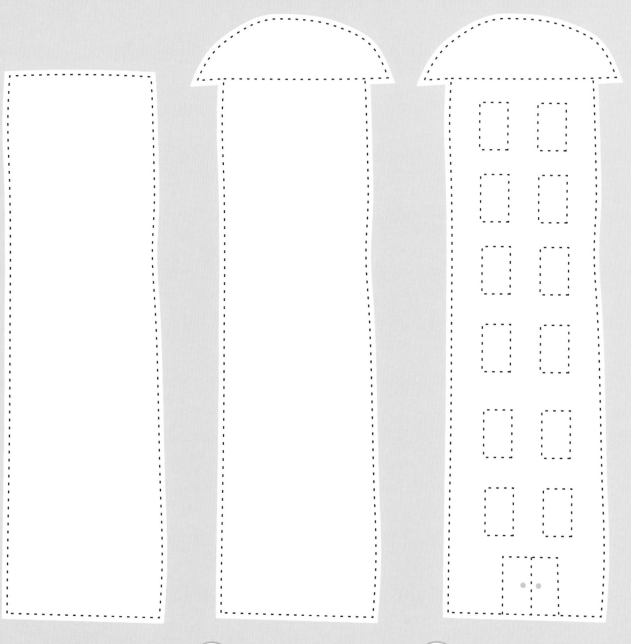

1. Start with a tall rectangle.

2. Add a roof at the top.

3. Finally, draw a lot of windows and a door.

Draw some skyscrapers by the road.

Let's Draw a Cat!

1. Draw a circle for the head.

2. Add ears, a nose, and a mouth.

3. Add eyes and whiskers.

4. Add a body.

5. Finally, draw legs and a tail.

Draw a cat standing in the window.
Is there more than one cat in the house?

Let's Draw a Butterfly!

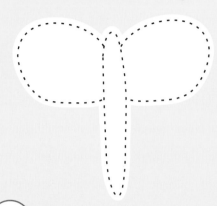

1. Start with a long oval for the body.

2. Add the tops of the wings.

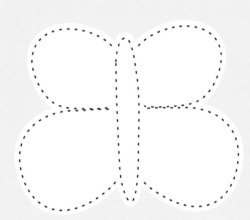

3. Add the bottoms of the wings.

4. Finally, draw a head and antennae.

5. What other details can you add?

Draw some butterflies in the sky.

Let's Draw a Flower!

1. Draw a circle for the center.

2. Add flower petals.

3. Draw a stem.

4. Finish by adding leaves.

Draw flowers in the grass.

Finish drawing the butterflies. Add details and color.

Draw the squirrel's tail. Next, draw some leaves and add color.

Draw wings on all the bees.
Add trails to show where they have flown.

Finish drawing the flowers. What color are they?
Add more bees.

Draw the snail's shell.

Add spots on the cows.

Draw more clouds in the sky.

Draw bows on the kite's tail.

Draw another snowman.

Draw more snowflakes.

Draw a plate with a piece of cheese.

Draw a tree, then add clouds and a sun.

Draw tops on the carrots.

Draw stripes and color the rainbow.

Finish the fence. What color should it be?

Draw more mud puddles and clouds.

Draw more tomatoes.

Draw a pretty sunrise.

Draw more leaves.

Draw more apples.

Let's Draw Faces!

Laughing   Surprised   Sleepy

Happy   Angry   Sad

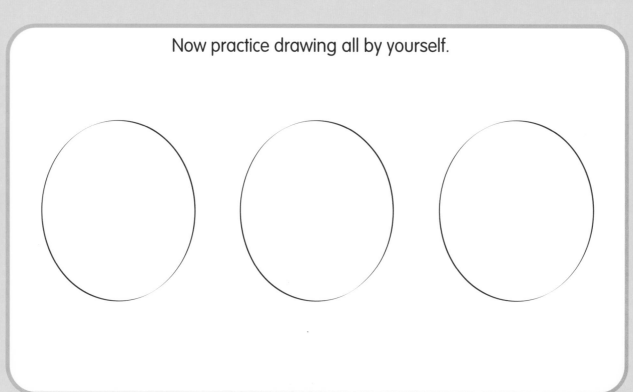

Now practice drawing all by yourself.

Draw a face.

Draw a face.

Draw a face.

Draw a face.

Draw a face.

Draw a face.

Draw a face.

Draw a face.

Draw a face.

Draw fruit in the bowl.

Draw boats in the water.

Draw a cake on a stand.

Draw a spaceship.

Draw flowers in the vase.

Draw stripes on the rainbow.

Draw a picture of your favorite toy.

Draw a picture of your favorite food.

Certificate of Achievement

I can DRAW!

Congratulations!

(name)

has successfully completed the FUN TO DRAW workbook

Presented on _____

Presented by _____

Certificate of Achievement

I learned a lot!

☐ I practiced holding a pencil.

☐ I drew lots of different things!

☐ I learned about shapes.

☐ I followed directions.

☐ I counted up to 10.

☐ I created some masterpieces!